HATERS

How Haters Are Born

Paul F. Davis

People are really good at being hateful and identifying haters (the latter being people who are hateful), but are not as discerning when it comes to discovering the origins and causes of their hate. I want to dig into the reasons people hate and how haters are born in this short book, as I have personally encountered people cross-culturally throughout the United States and around the world, whereby I have had countless opportunities to be offended and become a hater myself.

As an educator in a community of color, it is ironic how many times I get called the N word on a weekly basis (among other crude and vulgar things) by black teenagers.

Thus, part of cultural "sensitivity" is recognizing when a black person says something it is funny, but when a white person says the same thing, it is deemed rude and offensive. This gives me more respect for white comedians willing to approach (and sometimes cross) the line and be offensive, something I as an educator cannot do (as I'm only allowed to be a punching bag and endure the abuse, while being held to a higher standard).

I've collected a lot of material for stand-up comedy over the years by living abroad globally in every major continent around the world and in the United States while serving in ethnically diverse communities (Miami, San Francisco and LA) and having lived in NYC (Brooklyn and Queens) when I studied at NYU. Not to mention I lived with three gay guys (two of which were black) with whom I went to Bible College in southern California ironically.

Undoubtedly, people can be intense when pursuing their unique interests, trying to survive in this sometimes cold, cruel world and react with hostility when anyone gets in their way in route to where they are going.

Many in this generation have no filter whatsoever and immediately blurt out whatever is on their mind, regardless of the consequences and those they hurt along the way. This is unfortunate, but this does not mean we need to respond in similar fashion and match their cruelty and hostility.

As an international educator, I have lived in Florida (Orlando and Miami), New York (Brooklyn and Queens), Texas (Laredo near the border with Mexico) and California (San Francisco Bay Area, Los Angeles County and Orange County) within the United States. Overseas I have lived in Africa (Malawi, Burundi, Tanzania), Latin America (Guatemala and Chile), Europe (England) and Asia (China, India, Indonesia, Malaysia, Philippines, Vietnam, Taiwan and Hong Kong).

Moreover, I have traveled to 90 nations of the world, beyond those I have lived, studied and worked within. I have traveled from Mexico to Argentina, including having been twice to both Cuba and Venezuela. Although the American government often demonizes the governments of Cuba and Venezuela, I found the people there to be quite lovely. This is again another example of how you have to discern the difference between a nation's government, policies and people. My best friends are Latino and treat me like family.

As for Africa, I have been there on 5 tours and traveled to 8 nations. Incidentally, I have found the people of Africa to be nothing but lovely, warm and welcoming to me. My best friend from Bible College is black and my daughter calls him uncle.

Suffice it to say, I have interacted cross-culturally with innumerable people, some nicer than others and some rather rude and crude. Perhaps African Americans are more on edge, explosive and sensitive than Africans from the continent because of the inhumane and dehumanizing way historically they were treated in the United States. Healing old wounds does not occur easily, nor quickly. Therefore, we who call ourselves Americans must be extra patient and understanding with people of color and certain ethnicities, who have some fears and sensitivities our nation and its immoral government's policies historically helped to create. Changing and reforming laws is one thing, but reforming old mindsets and removing stinking thinking takes time to transform human beings.

Unkindness and disrespect is never easy to endure, but if we respond in a similar manner, it makes us no better than our haters. Of course, this is easier said than done during the heat of the moment when we are boiling with rage, becoming incensed with anger and are ready to erupt like a hot volcano.

Although most of us know this already, managing our emotions and remaining calm in intense interpersonal situations is not an easy task or accomplishment. Doing so however can make, break or transform a relationship (even alter the landscape of a non-existent relationship and set the stage for a friendship to begin, as many have testified who were willing to endure mistreatment and ultimately overcome evil with good).

Haters are born in the heat of the moment, often by multiple bad experiences with a particular person, or group of people, who disrespect, belittle or mistreat them. It can also occur when someone continually disagrees with a person or group of people and makes a sweeping judgment that ALL PEOPLE of a particular color, culture, country, religion, political persuasion or ideology are THE SAME, which most certainly they are not.

Hating one person is bad, but hating an entire group of people because of a lazy stereotypical attitude and sweeping judgment about an entire race, culture, country or group of people is horrible and dehumanizing.

Yet as I write in my book RACISM RULES, the person suffering the most from racism is ultimately the hater who cuts himself off from the wonderful blessings that befriending, cooperating and collaborating with people unlike him could bring into his life. People unlike us see things differently, have a unique perspective we can benefit from, and uncommon insights that can enlarge our vision and understanding, while enhancing and improving our people skills. All of these blessings can translate into better relationships with people, greater productivity and increased economic opportunities.

12 Ways Haters Are Born

1. When someone speaks harshly, impolitely or disrespectful to you.

We all have been spoken to inappropriately. Often it is not what is said, but more the way in which the words are spoken that agitate us and rub us the wrong way. Thereafter people commonly erect emotional walls of resistance to such a person who spoke to them in a hostile, or less than welcoming manner.

Sometimes such harsh communication was not done with any intention to harm whatsoever, but rather occurred out of common pursuits while trying to survive in this world.

Perhaps with a minimal amount of time during a lunch break, someone at the gas station honked their horn, hoping you would move your car out of the way so they could access the gasoline pump? Maybe they rolled their eyes in a time of frustration and said nothing whatsoever? Perhaps they spoke hastily and ill-advisedly, after which they regretted what they said, but by then had already driven away and did not know how to find you to apologize for their reckless words and impatient behavior.

Intentional disrespect coupled with arrogance and blatant defiance is totally different. I have experienced this often from teenage students (an age in and of itself that suddenly thinks they know it all) who did not want to comply with simple classroom rules (such as not eating in class, or not using their phones in class, or simply keeping their devices muted or using headphones). Complying with simple codes of conduct to exercise etiquette and manners is not something this generation is familiar with unfortunately and merely asking for some proper behavior can easily offend many in the younger generation.

Likewise, I see people at restaurants nowadays talking on their speaker phones with no regard for any other dining guests around them. I often will attempt to ask them (whoever they are and regardless of their color, political persuasion, or religion) to kindly turn off their volume, or talk outside. Most people in America are offended by this, although it is they who are behaving offensively and impolitely. The same situation in other countries, if and when it occurs, people are usually more inclined to acknowledge their inappropriate behavior and find another place to talk on their phone when confronted. Culture and parenting influences behavior, whether you want to acknowledge and admit it or not.

2. When someone behaves impolitely or disrespectfully to you.

I have had students of color say the most vile, crude, vulgar and disrespectful things imaginable (and beyond what most people can imagine and comprehend). Yet I am always willing to forgive them and move on daily.

Only the grace of Almighty God can soften my heart to forgive (and see each person through the loving heart and eyes of God) and be equitable toward those who mistreat and deeply offend me. In and of myself (without divine intervention), I will be equally as offended (or perhaps more) than anybody else.

Yet after some prayer and Bible reading, I am reminded that Jesus Christ my Savior died on the blood stained cross of Calvary with arms open wide and said, "Heavenly Father forgive them, for they do not know what they are doing" (Luke 23:34).

Likewise, I try, after I calm down following the heat of the moment, to be forgiving and gracious to people, remembering it is often not them speaking, but their demons raging within. People are a combined influence of their family, environment, upbringing and cultural influences. Thus, I do not allow students' vile speech and bad behavior to influence how I grade their academic work.

I recall once being at a Greyhound bus terminal in Orlando some 20 years ago, when I awaited the arrival of my bus to depart. While sitting in the lobby, I saw a black woman yelling and cursing at her two small children. The children looked to me to be no older than 2 or 3 years of age (so young, tender, precious and pure). Yet they were being cursed at with such hostility and intensity. That scene has never left my mind when I deal with people. We never know what people endured throughout their childhood, which shaped who they are today. Often the most unkind, cruel and unlovely people need the most love.

Only God Almighty can birth such a supernatural love in your heart (Romans 5:5) for such hardhearted and cruel people.

Ultimately, most people are merely reacting and responding to the environment they live in (or perceive themselves to be in) often feeling threatened, insecure, unloved and harshly treated themselves. Hence, they respond with hatred, bitterness and in an offensive manner which they feel is a defense mechanism (although it often further antagonizes and alienates the people they most need in their lives to support, assist and guide them).

Just remember that many who are disrespectfully shouting out (sometimes brutally, cruelly and with vulgarity) are often internally crying out for a father, mother and moral compass to be a light and source of guidance.

3. When someone inappropriately and incorrectly stereotypes, labels or judges you before they have taken the time to get to know you.

Making snap judgments is what lazy people, most people, unfortunately do. It is a survival mechanism by which people quickly try to discern and size up others, account for their environmental surroundings, and protect themselves despite the many unknowns all around. Very few people are patient and willing to slow down long enough to truly get to know a person, before making internal judgments about them based on their race, nationality, clothing, possessions, posture and manner of speech.

We all have haphazardly and recklessly internally made stereotypes about people we did not know. Fortunately, often when we have taken the time to truly get to know a person, we have proven our predispositions and snap judgments to be utterly wrong, inaccurate and entirely incorrect. Although we momentarily feel ashamed inside for incorrectly judging a person we did not yet know, we rarely admit to our folly and delay apologizing to the person outrightly.

Nevertheless, such moments of humility should be recollected and remembered before we fall prey to stereotypical internal dialogue and criticizing others within our hearts in the future before we have truly taken the time to get to know them and heard their life story.

Often it is difficult to get to know people when they erect walls, distance themselves from us due to past distrust or hurt from others. Yet as we remain patient, persistent and keep an open heart; eventually God will orchestrate situations whereby we can build bridges, connect and communicate with people to better get to know and understand them (and they us). Be patient. Life is a slow process, though hate can try to get us to move with haste. Hate is fast and furious. Love and peace is patient, believing, persistent and consistent.

4. When someone makes a blanket statement about a group of people which you are a part that you disagree with and consider false.

We cannot control the speech of others, but we can control how we respond to things we hear and do not agree with. Many things will be said throughout our lifetime, which we will not agree with. Yet this is not to say we must explode, react hastily and get pulled in emotionally to respond antagonistically, nor erect walls of division because of our disagreements. Disagreements are part of life and are not going anywhere, but we as people and fellow human beings can maintain a peaceful, welcoming disposition and remain agreeable when interacting with people with whom we disagree.

Remain calm and patient because surely there are points of agreement on which you can build and work to cooperate with every human being on some mutual interest to advance together.

Blanket statements are a sign of impatience, ignorance and intolerance for others. Yet calling an insecure and insensitive person out on their ignorance and err may not achieve the result you are looking for. Quite possibly by doing so, you will only arouse their insecurity and thereafter more hostility.

You have to sometimes be more subtle, gentle and clever in your approach to awaken a person to the error of their ways and the slippery slope on which they think, stand and are building their life.

Therefore, I recommend asking questions to such a person and hope God gives them wisdom and insight to awaken to the error of their ways. The light bulb may not come on during your discussions, interactions and questions. However, when the person is alone and able to reflect, ponder their past conversations and meditate on their daily interactions with others; it is then the Holy Spirit of God will shine the light on their life and help illuminate their mind. Therefore, be patient throughout the process and precise when asking probing questions to awaken those who are thinking and behaving incorrectly.

Some questions worthy of exploring, considering, asking or modifying slightly are:

- How long have you thought this way?

- Did you always think this way?

- What event or person caused you to begin to think this way?

- Did you ever have a conversation with the person after they offended you?

- How did that conversation and interaction go?

- Do you think and feel all people are the same? Why or why not?

- Would you be willing to teach your beliefs, ideas, biases, and prejudices to small children?

- What other things have you learned from your experiences?

- Are there any new insights you have learned lately that maybe do not align with your overall beliefs?

- When your experiences disagree and do not align with your beliefs, do you ever modify and change your beliefs to let go of your past prejudices to let new people have access to your life and be a blessing to you?

- What limitations are you putting on yourself (relationally, socially and professionally) by your present beliefs?

5. When someone disrespects or mistreats someone you love.

It is common and understandable for you to want to defend and stand up for those you love. We all have the tendency to do so. Yet what if the person we love and respect was partly to blame and showed some disrespect or poor behavior to antagonize and instigate others to have a beef (or problem) with them? In law, this is called contributory negligence, meaning a person had a part to play in the conflict and accident.

My mother was killed by an 18 year-old drunk driver at around 2am in the morning in Orlando, Florida, but she was drunk herself and had no business being out at 2am in the morning.

Likewise, we must be more honest and take accountability for the role we play in hostile communications and interactions with others. Emotions and feelings within erupt leading to wayward words and actions that do not always serve us well. Such toxic speech and behavior can result in interpersonal problems with people, parents, teachers, employers and the companies for whom we work. Regardless of how intelligent and talented you may be, if you cannot get along with people, many doors of opportunity will close on you throughout your life.

It takes time to develop self-esteem, self-control and people skills. Take some years to examine your heart, mind, thoughts and the way you interact with people.

As you do and embrace humility as a way of life, you will grow in self-awareness and improve your interactions and relationships with others, which simultaneously will result in more doors of opportunity opening to you and more financial blessings coming your way.

Mark my words, because if you heed my instruction, you will surely increase and be making more trips to the bank to cash in when you change how you think, relate, interact with, speak to and behave with others.

Consider everyone to be your sisters or brothers, aunties or uncles, mothers or fathers, grandmothers or grandfathers and your heart and mind will change, laying a pure foundation for proper interactions. Consider everyone to be in and a part of God's loving family, as this is the Creator's ultimate intention and desire for humanity to live together harmoniously.

6. When someone belittles and tries to manipulate and/or take advantage of you, assuming you are ignorant, unaware or will not somehow fight back.

I wrote two books titled ENERGIZED BY ANGER and ANGRY AT GOD & EVERYONE ELSE. I believe if utilized properly, anger can fuel your passion and purpose. Michael Jordan played basketball with a chip on his shoulder to prove his high-school basketball coach (who did not believe in him) wrong. During his Hall of Fame induction speech, Michael Jordan mentioned his high-school basketball coach as an influence that fueled his fire.

Two other NBA Hall of Fame basketball players, Kobe Bryant and Shaquille O'Neal had a rivalry sometimes fueled by anger, although they played on the same team together. Anger therefore does not always need to be negatively appropriated, but instead can be channeled if properly harnessed to motivate you to work hard, be better and achieve more.

Alternatively, if people who provoke and anger you become a mental distraction and poison you with offenses in your heart and mind, you will have difficulty concentrating on your purpose with purity and moving forward freely, because your soul will be contaminated with bitterness and hindered.

Lebron James talked about this when he won his first NBA championship with the Miami Heat. When the sports commentator interviewed him after he won the final game in the championship series, Lebron was asked: "What made this year different than last year?"

The Miami Heat made it to the finals the previous year, but lost. The following year in the championship finals, the Miami Heat won. Lebron therefore responded saying, "Last year I played with hate. I felt I had to prove myself. This year I played with love."

The internal mindset and difference in heart attitude elevated Lebron and the Miami Heat to play championship level basketball as they focused on their purpose, worked together as a team unit, and disregarded their haters, not allowing the hate and negativity (often spread through the media) to contaminate their souls, nor distract their focus.

Offenses are the bait of Satan (Genesis 4:1-7), whereby people are distracted from focusing on their purpose and diverted to fighting unnecessarily against one another. The best athletes understand that to perform at peak levels, they must disregard and block out the noise to focus on what they truly can do when competing in their sport.

Otherwise, mental and emotional distractions will weigh them down and prevent them from peak performance and high-level achievement.

7. When someone makes jokes or crude comments about you to entertain and humor his or her friends at your expense.

The bait of Satan will intensify the less focus, time, attention and emotionally invested you are in the criticism, cruel remarks and belittling words. People and demons hate to be ignored, demons even more so as it diminishes their effectiveness.

For demons to be successful in their Satanic attacks, they have to arouse your emotions, seduce you into their verbal exchange and thereafter slander and falsely accuse you. The devil in the Bible is known as a "murderer," the "father of lies" (John 8:44) and "the accuser" (Revelation 12:10) among other things. If you however remain silent and refuse to enter into such bickering and low-level conversation, the devil loses his power and has to find another way to engage you.

The devil comes to kill, steal and destroy your life (John 10:10). This can happen by stealing your time, attention, mental focus and emotional well-being through slanderous remarks, false accusations, vile and vulgar speech in an attempt to offend you and get you to fight with the people through whom Satan is speaking and operating to distract and wear you out.

8. When someone makes crude, cruel and unkind remarks about the people group you are a part of in your presence without any concern for your feelings.

I was riding the subway while living in New York City one Friday night, when across from me sat three African American guys making crude comments about their anatomy and implying anyone who was not black was inadequately endowed. I quietly sat and listened, while chuckling within, thinking to myself, if they were so manly, why were these three guys with one another and not with any ladies.

It just goes to show you that what a man (or at least one with the genitals physically) thinks to be important to get and keep a woman, is often different than what a woman wants in a man. Erroneous presumptions and predispositions abound among us whether in regard to gender, race, nationality, political persuasion, religious beliefs or some other ideology.

As for the crude and distasteful comments and jokes, you may be unable to stop them, but you most certainly can disregard them mentally and move yourself physically to sit, study, work and live elsewhere away from such people. I often say, "Show me your friends and I will show you your future."

After I moved to sit elsewhere on the train, I proceeded to read my book and enjoy the rest of my evening and weekend. This is the best way to respond to people trying to provoke you and arouse hatred within your heart. Don't succumb to Satanic seeds sown to grow within you feelings of superiority or inferiority. Instead live with purity and humility to find common ground and connect with humanity wholeheartedly and together live purposefully in harmony.

9. When people elevate their people group above yours and make self-exalting comments in your presence to subtly belittle you and attempt to make you feel inferior.

Siblings within families struggle with rivalries rooted in competition to claim superiority or respond to feelings of inferiority. The same happens within sports teams among athletes and in companies among executives and their employees. Therefore, it is not surprising there are competitive rivalries among people in society as they search for significant others romantically, status financially and to co-exist peacefully in the community when buying gasoline, shopping for groceries and necessities.

An array of attitudes abound given the time and season a person finds themselves in during their life. Likewise, people crossing paths in society or working together in a company may also manifest certain frustrations and hostilities. Strife is common to life and can be seen within families, when tensions rise, bills are not paid on time, dishes are not done, dinner is not cooked, and hostilities arise.

When we eat food, sometimes our teeth bite our tongue. Yet this is not reason to remove our teeth or tongue, as both serve a purpose and are needful. Likewise human beings must discern their strengths, talents and unique purposes to learn how to value one another and work together. This can be a time-consuming ordeal and agonizing process, which demands much patience.

However once embraced, it can yield a mutual respect, plan for partnership, commitment to cooperate and beautifully facilitate opportunities to increase in a multiplicity of ways ranging from finances to societal influence once teamwork is valued to make the dream work.

10. When people exercise physical violence, force or coercion to manipulate, punish and hurt you (or those you love).

Understandably, nobody likes those who exercise brute force against and bully them. As I write this book, Vladimir Putin of Russia has his countrymen going to war against neighboring Ukraine unnecessarily. I have been to both Ukraine and Russia. I love both countries. I have been to Russia twice and Ukraine several times. I am deeply saddened by the atrocities and inhumane treatment the Ukrainian people are having to endure, but I am proud of the Ukrainians for standing up to Putin and his vicious army trying to kill their people, remove their culture and steal their country. The Ukrainians have every reason to stand up to Russia and fight for their freedom.

I witnessed a similar situation in Timor Leste, formerly known as Timor Timor within Indonesia (a small island north of Darwin, Australia) where for 25 years Muslims within Indonesia were brutally mistreating, bullying and killing the Timorese. When they said enough is enough, stood up and fought for their independence, the Timorese gained their freedom and were recognized by the United Nations as a new nation. Yet it was a painful, bloody battle to fight and obtain their freedom.

Likewise in Africa, Rwandans and Burundians had to fight for their dignity when Hutus and Tutsis (two tribes) began fighting over their physical differences, skin color (though both are African), intelligence and other features compared and contrasted in 1994 on a local radio broadcast when one tribe began talking badly about the other. Soon thereafter the two tribes, who peacefully lived together for decades, took out their farming tools and used them to massacre 1.2 million people until the United Nations peacekeeping forces arrived to intervene.

Therefore, it is important to know what you are fighting for, who you are fighting and how best to fight. Killing one another does not change mindsets and the stinking thinking that instigated the strife to begin with.

America's costly wars in Vietnam, Iraq and Afghanistan are proof of this. None of these wars were truly won and everyone who fought in them on both sides of the world endured losses.

Alternatively, when you are attacked (as Ukraine has been by Russia) with military bombs, missiles and gunfire (along with being threatened with the likelihood of nuclear bombs to come in the future); at such a point there is little else to do than stand up and fight or leave the country altogether. Both options are certainly understandable, but fighting for the liberation of your homeland is the one most men would likely choose to secure the future for themselves and their families.

11. When people manipulate laws, societal systems, impose regulations, or covertly erect invisible barriers (perhaps through unseen networks and longstanding relationships) to discriminate and keep other people groups out.

Economic frustrations hindering mobility and an individual and his family from being able to sustain themselves in society (as during the Civil Rights movement when Dr. Martin Luther King and his leaders were denied hotel accommodations because they were black) are most certainly frustrating, aggravating and an understandable cause for growing bitter towards a people blocking

and hindering your progress in life and acceptance in the community.

It's not surprising the black community became frustrated when whites burned down black Wall Street in Tulsa, Oklahoma and sought to prevent their progress.

The documentary film KING IN THE WILDERNESS (available on HBO) about Dr. Martin Luther King following his assassination, mentioned real estate brokers in Chicago preventing blacks from moving into certain neighborhoods. Such institutional and economic racism can be terribly frustrating and infuriating, by which people of color come to hate the white people (or those they perceive to be) preventing their progress and integration into a community. Thereafter feelings of hatred toward

ALL WHITE PEOPLE easily follow, although they may not be justifiable.

Nevertheless, despite the cruelty of discrimination, as Michelle Obama has stated, the best way to respond to low blows of racism, discrimination and inhumanity is to "go higher" and live by God's law of love to demonstrate a better way, overcoming evil with good to silence your critics by good behavior and respectfully living a life of dignity.

People will not always understand you, but if you live with integrity and demonstrate morality and upright character, you will not be able to be spoken evil of, which over time, surely will cause you to win some hearts and minds. As you do, you can build a constituency of friends, allies and

advocates to favor and fight for your cause and the advancement of your people alongside you.

The march for justice and equality may seem long, laborious and like a heavy cross to carry, but going about it the right way will silence your enemies and win many to stand with you in truth for justice to do that which is right. Alternatively, responding hatefully and violently, will tarnish your name, reputation, credibility and delay any lasting progress whatsoever while creating more enemies. Love and peace always win. Although they seem to move a bit slower, they are most certainly sustainable.

12. When an individual or people group exclude, alienate, or oppress another people group (or individuals in that people group) to advance or protect their interests at the expense of the other people group, making it difficult for all to peaceably and harmoniously co-exist.

Being excluded, dehumanized, or chosen last on a sports team of athletes all can be demoralizing and belittling experiences. Yet as you hold your head up high and choose to not be poisoned by hate, God will bring true friends to you and you will progress with people of like precious faith with pure mindsets and beliefs.

Rather than fight enemies, make friends with the pure in heart and work together skillfully and strategically to overcome evil with good, silence your skeptics and critics, and win people to favor and advance your just cause.

Wisdom is more powerful, influential and sustainable than raw hard power, rude speech and impatient slander belittling people. Dirty politicians willing to slander their opponent never win much respect from people at large and their careers are short-lived being unsustainable. Successful people know how to work with others, especially people who are different from them. Because we all have common ground, mutual interests and causes we value and can cooperate on to advance.

If we would simply communicate more with one another, listen to each other's concerns, and consider one another's interests; we will be more able to cooperatively advance and collectively harness our strengths for mutual benefit. Our purposes are often common and intersect in some way. Find the point(s) of agreement and work together with people who value your causes and initiatives.

Dr. Martin Luther King found a friend in the Vietnamese, who he refused to go to war with. Instead, Dr. King chose to be a peacemaker and not support an unjust war in Vietnam, despite many Republicans supporting the war effort.

For this reason, the Federal Bureau of Investigation (FBI) spied on Dr. King and his wife (wiretapping their phones) for 4 years (after MLK's assassination) to listen in on their conversations to ensure they did not interfere with the war in Vietnam.

Work and fight smarter, because this is the best way to outsmart and beat your enemies. The war for hearts and minds requires skill and soft power. The more accurate and skillful you are as an orator, communicator, mediator able to resolve conflict and peacemaker to calm nerves; the more effective you will be at influencing and persuading people to see your point of view and favor your cause.

Dr. Martin Luther King protested outside of real estate brokerages in Chicago to capture media attention and awaken citizens to the unethical treatment African Americans were enduring when seeking to look for and buy a home in their city. By shining the light on evildoers and peacefully confronting injustice, Dr. King was able to get the media and some people of Chicago on his side to increase his influence and economically appeal to real estate brokers by showing African Americans had money in hand and were ready to buy property if given the chance to do so. Thus Dr. King peacefully outsmarted his enemies, built on the civil rights movement in Chicago to gain for his people credibility, and thereby altered the rules to buy property and make the playing field more level for all home buyers.

13. Hate is also birthed by insecurity and jealousy, when you feel inferior in the presence of another person.

Feelings of inferiority and insecurity that arouse jealousies and thereafter a subconscious hatred of a person; often have nothing to do with the person, but your assessment of yourself and response to them as you compare yourself. If another person's greatness, gifts, talents, abilities, possessions, wealth, ability to communicate effectively and fluently, people skills, intelligence or athleticism make you feel inferior; then you have unfinished business to attend to regarding your own self-esteem. Your insecurity and jealousy have everything to do with your self-image, self-esteem (or lack thereof) and assessment of yourself.

Projecting your insecurities and jealousies on to someone else to cloud the real issue, how you feel about and see yourself, will never identify, address, nor solve the true problem.

Such a person needs to go to God in prayer, read His Word (the Bible) and awaken to the fact that all human beings are created in the image and likeness of God (Genesis 1:26-28), each having his own distinct gifts, talents and abilities. Therefore, rather than focusing on what you don't have, it is in your best interest to focus on what you do have, be thankful for and cultivate that. Attend to that which God has given and graced you with, rather than unwisely comparing yourself with others

(2Corinthians 10:12), which only leads to feelings of superiority or inferiority.

Pride and insecurity are power depleting attitudes of the heart, which distract your focus as they pull your eyes off your purpose and instead place them on yourself or others.

If you enjoyed and were blessed by this book, please contact Paul to share your kind comments and a positive testimony. If you would like to make arrangements to have Paul speak in your city, please kindly email him to do so.

PaulFDavis.com

EducationPro.us

PropheticPowerShift.com

RevivingNations@yahoo.com

Tinyurl.com/PaulFDavis-Books